JOURNAL

PETER PAUPER PRESS, INC.
WHITE PLAINS, NEW YORK

PETER PAUPER PRESS
Fine Books and Gifts Since 1928

Our Company

In 1928, at the age of twenty-two, Peter Beilenson began printing books on a small press in the basement of his parents' home in Larchmont, New York. Peter—and later, his wife, Edna—sought to create fine books that sold at "prices even a pauper could afford."

Today, still family owned and operated, Peter Pauper Press continues to honor our founders' legacy—and our customers' expectations—of beauty, quality, and value.

Cover image copyright © 2010 Josephine Wall
All rights reserved

Josephine Wall, whose paintings are well-loved the world over,
paints in her cottage studio in Dorset, England.
Her passion for nature and myth resonate in her intricately
detailed artwork that weaves together the romantic and the surreal.

Copyright © 2010
Peter Pauper Press, Inc.
202 Mamaroneck Avenue
White Plains, NY 10601
All rights reserved
ISBN 978-1-4413-0263-2
Printed in China
14 13

Visit us at www.peterpauper.com